Collins Primary Literacy

Pupil Book 5

Kay Hiatt and Mary Green
Series editor: Kay Hiatt

Published by Collins
An imprint of HarperCollins*Publishers*
77–85 Fulham Palace Road
Hammersmith
London
W6 8JB

© HarperCollins*Publishers* Limited 2008

Authors: Kay Hiatt and Mary Green

Series editor: Kay Hiatt

10 9 8 7 6 5 4

ISBN 978 0 00 722699 3

British Library Cataloguing in Publication Data
A Catalogue record for this publication is available from the British Library.

Acknowledgements
The authors and publishers wish to thank the following for permission to use copyright material:
Unit 1: Michael Morpurgo for text from *Billy the Kid* by Michael Morpurgo (Pavilion Books); Michael Morpurgo for text from *The Dancing Bear* by Michael Morpurgo (Young Lions); Michael Morpurgo for text from *Kensuke's Kingdom* (Heinemann Young Books); Michael Morpurgo for text from *The Dancing Bear* (HarperCollins); Unit 3: Penguin Books for use of "Talking Turkeys", "Who's Who" and "A Day in the Life of Danny the Cat" from *Talking Turkeys* by Benjamin Zephaniah, text © Benjamin Zephaniah, 1994 (Viking); "Winter" text © Judith Nicholls 1987, from *Midnight Forest* by Judith Nicholls (Faber and Faber Limited) reprinted with kind permission of the author; Unit 4: Usborne Publishing Limited for text from *The Usborne Book of Greek and Norse Legends*, © Usborne Publishing Limited; Laura Cecil Literary Agency on behalf of the James Reeves Estate for text from *Giants and Warriors* by James Reeves, text © James Reeves, 1977 (Blackie & Son); Unit 5: Attic Media for text from *National Geographic Kids* March 2007 for *On top of the world*; Unit 6: PFD on behalf of the Estate of Hilaire Belloc for use of *Matilda* from *The Bad Child's Book of Beasts* by Hilaire Belloc, text © The Estate of Hilaire Belloc, 1896; Unit 7: Roald Dahl for text from *The BFG – plays for children* by Roald Dahl, adapted by David Wood (Puffin); Jane Serraillier Grossfield for use of "The Visitor" by Ian Serraillier, text © The Estate of Ian Serraillier (from *A Second Poetry Book* edited by John Foster, OUP 1980); Unit 9: Unitec AG & German Film School for film stills from *The Beauty of Life*, © Unitec AG & German Film School; Unit 10: PFD on behalf of the author for text from *Tukku-Tukku and Samson* from *A Thief in the Village and Other Stories* by James Berry, text © James Berry, 1989; Unit 11: Gallimard Jeunesse for text and illustrations from *The Little Prince* by Antoine de Saint-Exupéry (Wordsworth Classics); Unit 12: Walker Books Limited for use of "The Pow-wow Drum" from *A Carribean Dozen* by David Campbell, edited by John Agard and Grace Nicols, text © David Campbell, 1994.

Illustrations: Peter Bull, Brenda McKetty, Jo Taylor, Paul McCaffrey, Harris Sofokleous, Tim Archbold, Julia Pearson, Mark Oldroyd

Photographs: p9, top left: FLPA/Silvestris Fotoservice, top right: FLPA/Frans Lanting, bottom: FLPA/Minden Pictures/Jim Brandenburg; p11: Alamy/Lee Hacker; p14, top: Alamy/Yuri Afanasiev, centre left: Alamy/ F1 online, centre right: Alamy/Travelshots.com, bottom left: Alamy/Chris A. Crumley, bottom centre: Alamy/Nordicphotos, bottom right: Alamy/Loolee, bottom right inset: Alamy/Dennis Hallinan; p15, left: Alamy/Daniel Goodchild, top right: Alamy/Brian Harris, bottom right: Alamy/Rob Wilkinson; p17: Alamy/ Jeff Morgan Hay on Wye; p29: www.180degrees.co.uk; p31, top and bottom: Getty Images News/Joe Raedle; p32: Alamy/Kos Picture Source; p37: FLPA/Minden Pictures/Jim Brandenburg; p60: Alamy/Visual Arts Library; p61, top left: Alamy/Visual Arts Library, centre left: Alamy/Glyn Thomas, bottom left: Corbis/Mimmo Jodice, bottom right: Alamy/Visual Arts Library; p63, left and top right: Alamy/Visual Arts Library

Browse the complete Collins catalogue at
www.collinseducation.com

Printed in Hong Kong by Printing Express Ltd

Mixed Sources
Product group from well-managed forests and other controlled sources
www.fsc.org Cert no. SW-COC-1806
© 1996 Forest Stewardship Council

FSC is a non-profit international organisation established to promote the responsible management of the world's forests. Products carrying the FSC label are independently certified to assure consumers that they come from forests that are managed to meet the social, economic and ecological needs of present and future generations.

Find out more about HarperCollins and the environment at
www.harpercollins.co.uk/green

Contents

Michael Morpurgo

In this unit, you'll read Michael Morpurgo's novel, *Kensuke's Kingdom*, and look at other stories he's written.

Openings

Here are the openings to three of Michael Morpurgo's novels.

Kensuke's Kingdom

I disappeared on the night before my twelfth birthday. July 28 1988. Only now can I at last tell the whole extraordinary story, the true story.

from Kensuke's Kingdom
by Michael Morpurgo

Billy the Kid

I shouldn't have been here really, not by rights. I should've been pushing up the daisies a long time ago. But I'm not, I'm here, and I'm eighty years old, eighty years old today.

from Billy the Kid
by Michael Morpurgo

The Dancing Bear

I was born in this mountain village longer ago than I care to remember. I was to have been a shepherd like my grandfather and his grandfather before him, but when I was three, an accident left me with a limp.

from The Dancing Bear
by Michael Morpurgo

1 Read/pair/share

Read the story openings quietly to yourself. Then get into pairs and take turns to read the openings to each other. Read them as if you were the character talking to a friend.

2 Writing in the first person

Michael Morpurgo makes it seem as if a person inside the story is telling it to you. So, instead of writing:

> *The boy sat under the leafy tree.*

Michael Morpurgo would write:

> *I sat under the leafy tree.*

Using "I" brings the reader close to a character. This is called writing in the *first person*.

1 Rewrite the story opening below in the first person:

> *The boy sat under the leafy tree. He was looking after his mother's new baby, and feeling very sorry for himself.*
>
> *Suddenly he heard a strange whirring sound coming from the tree above him – what could it be? He stood up to have a look and was shocked by what he saw…*

2 Now continue the passage, writing in the first person.

The Village Teacher

The opening pages of The Dancing Bear *tell the reader a lot about the teacher, and about Michael Morpurgo's views on him.*

I was born in this mountain village longer ago than I care to remember. I was to have been a shepherd like my grandfather and his grandfather before him, but when I was three, an accident left me with a limp. Shepherding wasn't ever going to be possible, so I became a teacher instead.

For nearly forty years now, I have been the schoolmaster here. I live alone in a house by the school, content with my own company and my music. To play my hunting horn high in the mountains, and to hear its echo soaring with the eagles, is as close as I have been to complete happiness.

Yet I suppose you could say that I became a sort of shepherd after all: I shepherd children instead of sheep, that's all. I teach them, and I'm a kind of uncle to them even after they've left school. They think I'm a bit eccentric – I play my horn and I talk to myself more than I should. Like all children, they can be a bit cruel from time to time. They call me "Three Legs" or "Long John Silver" when they think I'm not listening, but you have to put up with that.

We are people whose lives are ruled by sheep, by the seasons, and above all by the mountains. We make cheese here, sheep's cheese. You won't find a better cheese anywhere, that's a promise. Almost all the families have a flock of sheep which they graze in the fields around the village, but when the snows clear, they take them up on to the mountain pastures for the sweet summer grass. The cows go too, and the horses and the pigs.

Snow cuts us off for at least three months of every winter, sometimes more, and then we are left to ourselves. But it's a peaceful place at any time of year. The winding road from the valley ends in the village square. Beyond us are the mountains, and beyond the mountains, the sky. We are a world of our own and we like it that way. We are used to it. The life is hard but predictable. People are born, people die. We have our blizzards and our droughts, no one ever has enough money and the roof always needs repairing.

from **The Dancing Bear** *by Michael Morpurgo*

3 Responding to the text

Read *The Village Teacher* again. Do you agree or disagree with the sentences below? Give reasons for your answers (the first one is done for you).

1. The teacher wishes he was younger.

   I agree with this sentence because he says that he was born "longer ago than I care to remember".

2. He would have preferred to be a shepherd than a teacher.

3. He enjoys the company of his friends.

4. He doesn't like being called names.

5. He's proud of the cheese which is made in the village.

6. He's unhappy about having to live in the village.

7. Michael Morpurgo allows you to get to know the character's feelings.

8. Decide which of these views you agree with and give your reasons:

   a) Michael Morpurgo is trying to make you dislike the teacher.

   b) Michael Morpurgo is trying to make you like the teacher.

4 Learning more about Michael

Read the opening of *Kensuke's Kingdom*, up to *They both tried to find other jobs, but there was nothing*. Find evidence that gives you answers to these questions (the first one is done for you).

① Can Michael keep a secret? How do you know?

We know this because he says that ten years had passed, showing that he has told no one about Kensuke. This shows he can be trusted – he can keep a secret.

② Does Michael respect Kensuke?

③ What does Michael say about Stella that shows that he loves her?

④ What did Michael enjoy about playing a football match on the recreation ground?

⑤ Did Michael save his money?

⑥ What did Michael love about sailing?

⑦ Did Michael show off sometimes?

5 Planning a survival story

Plan and write your own survival story. It should be about a child who is separated from their parents. The story should show how brave the child is in a difficult situation. You'll need to:

- choose a setting.

- plan some dramatic events.

- show how the child overcomes dangers and survives.

6 Writing a survival story

Now write your story.

- Tell the story so that it captures the interest of your reader. Use what you have learned about Michael Morpurgo's writing style to do this.

- Tell your story in the first person, using the voice of the child who is lost.

- Use repetition.

- Make your character speak directly to the reader.

- Make sure the reader really knows how your character feels.

Writer's guide

☑ **Write!**
Don't forget to add punctuation as you go along!

☑ **Read!**
Does it make sense? Is it interesting? Is it exciting?

☑ **Reread!**
Which parts read well? Which parts can you get rid of?

☑ **Rewrite!**
Check spellings and punctuation. Add words and phrases to bring your story to life.

☑ **Share with a friend!**
Can they identify with the character's situation? Can they picture where the character is?

What I have learned

- I understand what makes Michael Morpurgo a significant author.

- I can identify the themes, characters and settings of his novels.

- I can empathise with characters through role play.

- I can identify dramatic events in a story.

How to Have Fun!

In this unit, you'll look at recipes and instructions in everyday life. You'll organise a Fun Day, and write instructions for the games and activities.

Recipes

This recipe is written in informal English and uses slang expressions.

Orange juice

Orange juice

FRESH AND FAB ORANGE JUICE!
This is an easy recipe that tastes wicked!

You will need:

- 12 juicy oranges
- an electric orange juicer or an orange squeezer.

Method

Cut the oranges in half on a board. Squeeze each orange half using an electric juicer or an orange squeezer.

Pour the juice into a jug. Chuck in a handful of ice cubes – dead cool!

1 Think/pair/share

1. Make a note of the slang expressions used in this recipe.

2. Here are some more expressions:

   slap   slop   whack   Get stuck in!   There you go!

   How would these words be used in a recipe?

3. Think of more formal words to replace these expressions.

Recipe for Making Adults Cross

This poem uses the recipe format in a humorous way.

Offer to go shopping with a parent.
Don't take no for an answer.
Halfway to the bus stop remember about the tap
    you left running in the bathroom.
Back at the house remember that you turned it
    off after all.
Catch the next bus.
 Ask why this bus is going the wrong way.
 Get off bus.
Mention that you should have brought
    an umbrella.
Wait exactly one hour for next bus.
 Stand up all the way to town.
  After ten minutes in town remember that you
     hate shopping even more than
      watching "Newsround".
  Mention this ten or eleven times in a loud voice.
  Keep very quiet for next half hour.
  Walk slowly.
 Walk more slowly.
Stop walking, ask to go to the toilet.
Walk very fast for up to an hour looking for one.
Offer to carry a bag. Swing bag.
Look surprised when handle breaks.
Catch bus home. About a mile from home
    mention that you feel a bit sick.
Get off bus.
 As bus drives away say that you feel
    all right now.
 Mention that you should have
    brought an umbrella (and a torch).
Keep quiet for next two days.

                 Martyn Wiley

2 Responding to the text

Answer the questions from the , or section.

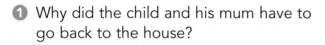
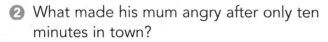

1. Why did the child and his mum have to go back to the house?

2. What made his mum angry after only ten minutes in town?

3. Why did the handles break on the bag?

4. Why did they get off the bus?

5. Write down what his mum might have said to him when he mentioned that she should have brought an umbrella and a torch.

6. Why do you think he kept quiet for the next two days?

7. Is this a funny poem?

1. Which features of a recipe can you spot?

2. Why is the poem laid out in a series of separate sentences?

3. What kind of child never takes no for an answer?

4. Which event in the day would you consider to be the worst one for Mum? Say why.

5. Do you think Martyn Wiley might have children of his own? Why do you think that?

6. Why do you think the child kept quiet for the next two days?

7. Do you think this is a funny poem?

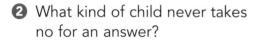

1. Which features of a recipe can you spot?

2. What kind of child never takes no for an answer?

3. Write down what Mum thought when they had to return home.

4. What would have made her even more cross before they reached town?

5. Which lines in the poem tell us the child doesn't like shopping?

6. Why do you think he kept quiet for the next two days?

7. Is this a funny poem?

Wish you were here?

This text uses a recipe to sell a holiday.

The Recipe for a Perfect Holiday

Ingredients

- Sunny weather
- Private beach
- Waiter service
- Award-winning beach restaurant
- Luxurious hotel

Method

1. Contact us at our email address.
2. Tell us when you want to go.
3. Buy some holiday clothes.
4. Pack your bags.
5. Enjoy your first-class flight.
6. Relax!

3 Independent writing

1. Read *The Recipe for a Perfect Holiday*.

2. Now create your own recipe for your dream holiday. These pictures might give you some ideas.

Plan a school Fun Day

Your class is going to organise a school Fun Day. Draw up a plan for the day.
Include different activities, games and events. Look at the list below
for some ideas.

- mass warm-up
- fun run, runners dressed as a character from a book or film
- egg-and-spoon relay race
- obstacle race
- throw the boot – throwing the boot as far as you can
- keep the ball in the air – beach game
- dressing-up race
- cookery demonstrations
- leap frog
- treasure hunt
- silly golf – play golf with your feet
- blow the biggest bubble
- bouncing balls around obstacles
- skipping races
- three-legged race
- sack race
- coconut shy

4 Writing instructions

1. Choose which games you want to write instructions for.

2. Plan the sequence of steps for each game.

3. Write a list of instructions for each game.

4. Try out each game, following your instructions. (If there is time, ask another group to try them.) Change them if you need to.

5. Now demonstrate your games to the class.

What I have learned

- I can write a clear set of instructions.
- I understand that instructions can be written in a more informal style.
- I can use slang to change the style of a recipe.

Remember!

A good recipe or set of instructions:

- allows you to make or do something successfully.

- is written in the present tense and use imperative verbs, like "take" and "cut".

- has a clear purpose – to get something done.

- is written for an adult, a child or both.

Poets with Passion

In this unit, you'll explore the poetic styles of two different poets, and then create your own free-verse poem.

Benjamin Zephaniah is famous for writing poems, and for performing them. This poem is written exactly as if he was speaking the words.

Talking Turkeys

Be nice to yu turkeys dis Christmas
Cos' turkeys just wanna hav fun
Turkeys are cool, turkeys are wicked
An every turkey has a mum.
Be nice to yu turkeys dis Christmas,
Don't eat it, keep it alive,
It could be yu mate, an not on your plate
Say, "Yo! Turkey I'm on your side."
I got lots of friends who are turkeys
An all of dem fear Christmas time,
Dey wanna enjoy it, dey say humans destroyed it
An humans are out of dere mind,
Yeah, I got lots of friends who are turkeys
Dey all hav a right to a life,
Not to be caged up an genetically made up
By any farmer an his wife.

Benjamin Zephaniah

Who's Who

I used to think **nurses**
Were women,
I used to think **police**
Were men,
I used to think **poets**
Were boring,
Until **I** became one of **them**.

Benjamin Zephaniah

1 Read/pair/share

Read the verse from *Talking Turkeys* together. Discuss these questions:

- What do you think the poem is about?

- What do you think the poem's message is?

- How is the poem written? Is it a rhyme or a rap? Is it serious or funny?

- What accent should it be read in? What's different about the spelling?

A Day in the Life of Danny the Cat

Benjamin Zephaniah has observed his cat carefully in order to write this poem.

Danny wakes up
Eats
Finds a private place in the garden,
He returns
Plays with plants
And sleeps.

Danny wakes up
Eats
Inspects the garden
Finds a cosy place
And sleeps.

Danny wakes up
Comes indoors
Inspects the carpet
Scratches himself
And sleeps.

Danny wakes up
Goes in the garden
Over the fence
Has a fight with Ginger
Makes a date with Sandy
Climbs on to next door's shed
And sleeps.

Danny wakes up
Comes indoors
Rubs up the chair leg
Rubs up a human leg
Sharpens his claws
On a human leg
Eats
And sleeps.

Danny wakes up
Eats
Watches a nature programme
Finds a private place in the garden,
Finds Sandy in next door's garden
Next door's dog finds Danny
Sandy runs north
Danny runs home
Eats an sleeps.

Danny wakes up
Checks for mice
Checks for birds
Checks for dogs
Checks for food
Finds a private place
in the garden
Eats
And sleeps.

Danny has hobbies,
Being stroked
Car watching
And smelling feet
He loves life,
Keeps fit
And keeps clean,
Every night he covers himself
In spit,
Then he eats
And sleeps.

Benjamin Zephaniah

2 Responding to the text

Answer questions from the , or section.

1 How does the poet know so much about his cat?

2 Why does he keep using the phrase *Danny wakes up*?

3 Why does Danny like to find a private place in the garden?

4 What does he enjoy doing inside?

5 Is the poet showing his love for animals in this poem?

6 Do you love an animal enough to write a poem about it?

1 How does the poet know so much about his cat?

2 Make a list of Danny's favourite activities.

3 What is Danny doing when he covers himself in spit?

4 Is Danny a well-loved cat? How do you know this?

5 Why is the style of this poem so different from *Talking Turkeys*?

6 Do you love an animal enough to write a poem about it?

1 How does the poet know so much about his cat?

2 Why does he keep using the phrase *Danny wakes up*?

3 Does Danny prefer Ginger or Sandy? Say why.

4 Does Danny prefer being inside or outside?

5 Find one word to describe Danny's feelings about life.

6 Do you love an animal enough to write a poem about it?

Winter

Judith Nicholls writes about how the landscape changes in the winter.

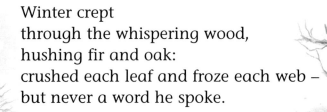

Winter crept
through the whispering wood,
hushing fir and oak:
crushed each leaf and froze each web –
but never a word he spoke.

Winter prowled
by the shivering sea,
lifting sand and stone;
nipped each limpet silently –
and then moved on.

Winter raced
down the frozen stream,
catching at his breath;
on his lips were icicles,
at his back was death.

Judith Nicholls

3 Group discussion

Talk about what is happening in the poem, thinking about the points listed below.

1. Discuss the way Judith Nicholls writes about winter as if he is a person, rather than a season. For example, she calls winter *he* all the way through the poem.

2. Judith Nicholls describes this as a "mysterious poem". Which words does she use to create a mysterious atmosphere? Search through the poem carefully and write a list of these.

3. Mysterious things happen in this poem. How do you think winter can hush a wood and crush leaves? How do you think he can lift sand and stone?

4 Independent activity

1 Show how winter transforms autumn scenes by drawing six pictures side by side:

the wood on an autumn day	→	the wood on a winter's day
the shoreline on an autumn day	→	the shoreline on a winter's day
a stream on an autumn day	→	a stream on a winter's day

2 Draw a picture of what you imagine winter to look like, based on this poem.

5 Collecting ideas for an animal poem

You're going to write a poem about a pet or another animal that you like, and that you have observed carefully. Begin by thinking about the things you want to tell your reader about your animal, for example:

- the animal's name and age
- where it lives
- what it eats
- what it likes to do every day
- special things you like about it

- something surprising that may have happened to it
- if it is your pet, why you love it
- if it is an endangered animal, why it needs the reader's help.

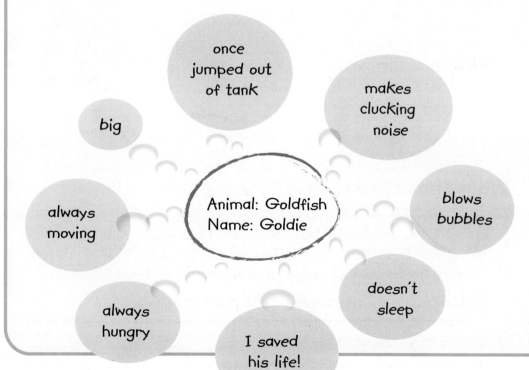

once jumped out of tank

makes clucking noise

big

Animal: Goldfish
Name: Goldie

always moving

blows bubbles

always hungry

I saved his life!

doesn't sleep

6 Writing a free-verse poem

Use your ideas to write some sentences about your animal. Make the sentences sound like poetry. You could include:

- images that will create a picture in the reader's mind.
- words and phrases that will get your message across to the reader.

When you have a few sentences, experiment with laying them out as a poem. You could write your poem as a series of sentences, like this:

> Goldie Goldfish swims around, all day long.
> He's always on the move, he never sleeps.
> He's always hungry, a big fish!
> When he blows bubbles, he makes a clucking sound like a bird.
> Once he jumped out of his tank, but I saved him – and then I knew how
>   much I loved him.

Or you could break your sentences up to make verses, like this:

> Goldie Goldfish swims around, on the move, never sleeps, all day long.
>
> Enormous for his age,
> always starving,
> blows bubbles,
> sounds like a bird!
>
> Saved him once,
> then I knew
> how much I really loved him.

What I have learned

- I can comment on the style of a poem and its message.
- I can compare two poems by different poets on similar themes.
- I appreciate that not all poems rhyme.
- I can write a piece of free verse about a living creature.

Monsters and Myths

In this unit, you'll learn about monster characters in Greek myths and create your own monster for a new myth.

Amazing Monsters

Greek monsters are gruesome characters assembled from bits and pieces of other creatures! These are some of the many monsters from Greek myths.

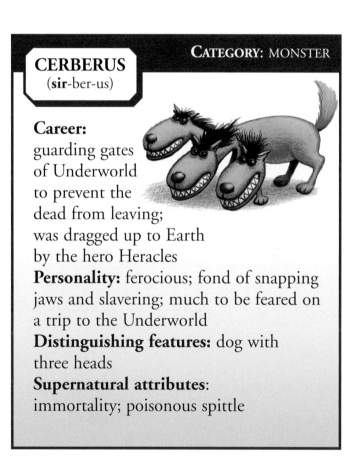

CERBERUS
(**sir**-ber-us)

CATEGORY: MONSTER

Career: guarding gates of Underworld to prevent the dead from leaving; was dragged up to Earth by the hero Heracles
Personality: ferocious; fond of snapping jaws and slavering; much to be feared on a trip to the Underworld
Distinguishing features: dog with three heads
Supernatural attributes: immortality; poisonous spittle

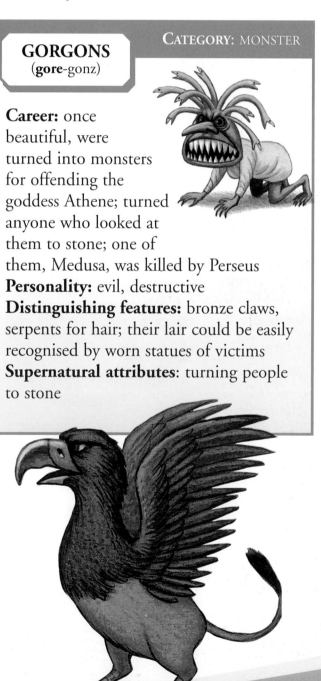

GORGONS
(**gore**-gonz)

CATEGORY: MONSTER

Career: once beautiful, were turned into monsters for offending the goddess Athene; turned anyone who looked at them to stone; one of them, Medusa, was killed by Perseus
Personality: evil, destructive
Distinguishing features: bronze claws, serpents for hair; their lair could be easily recognised by worn statues of victims
Supernatural attributes: turning people to stone

HARPIES
(**har**-peez)

Career: pestering human victims by stealing their food and screeching so that they cannot sleep

Personality: nasty; persistent and tireless; extremely unwelcome visitors

Distinguishing features: birds with nagging, female heads

Supernatural attributes: flying and nagging abilities in deadly combinations

MANTICORE
(**man**-tee-core)

CATEGORY: MONSTER

Career: a man-eating fabulous beast from Persia. First mentioned in the fifth century BC in a Greek history of Persia

Personality: vicious, merciless

Distinguishing features: head of a man with three rows of teeth; body of a lion with porcupine's quills; scorpion's tail

Supernatural attributes: the sting on its tail can be shot like an arrow

SIRENS
(**sye**-runs)

CATEGORY: MONSTER

Career: singing to lure sailors onto the rocks, and wrecking their ships; only Jason and Odysseus ever escaped

Personality: destructive, wicked

Distinguishing features: very beautiful female faces and voices; bird-like bodies with wings and claws

Supernatural attributes: their voices, which are irresistible to humans

MINOTAUR
(**my**-no-tore)

CATEGORY: MONSTER

Career: lived in Labyrinth designed by Daedalus; ate human flesh; killed by Theseus

Personality: evil, murderous, full of hatred

Distinguishing features: head and shoulders of a bull, body of a man

Supernatural attributes: fantastic strength and devouring ability

adapted from **The Usborne Book of Greek and Norse Legends**

1 Responding to the text

Answer the questions from the , or  section.

❶ How were the Sirens dangerous to sailors?

❷ How can you tell when you've found the Gorgons' lair?

❸ What would help the Manticore in a battle with a Greek hero?

❹ Choose which monster would frighten you the most, and write down the reasons why.

❶ What do the following words and phrase mean? Use a dictionary if you need to.

| devouring | ordinary mortals |
| lethal |

❷ Which do you think is the strongest – the Cerberus or a Gorgon? Explain your answer.

❸ List three reasons why you wouldn't want to meet a Harpy.

❹ Choose which monster would frighten you the most, and write down the reasons why.

❶ What do the following words and phrase mean? Use a dictionary if you need to.

| immortality | irresistibly attractive |
| hideous |

❷ Which is the least dangerous of the monsters? Explain why.

❸ Which monster would make the best pet? Write down the reasons why.

❹ Choose one of the monsters and explain what you would do if you met it.

Theseus and the Minotaur

Ariadne is the daughter of King Minos. She is standing by the quay when the seven maidens and seven youths are brought from Greece to be fed to the monstrous Minotaur. She instantly falls in love with one of the youths, the handsome Theseus, and decides she must save him from the monster.

"Handsome Athenian, I am grieved that you and your companions must be sacrificed tomorrow. It is a terrible thing."

"Then ask your father to spare us," said Theseus.

"He will not listen to me. He is stern and revengeful. Every year it has been my unhappy lot to see your young men and maidens go away to be slain by the Minotaur. My father will only say that the monster, which is sacred, must have human victims."

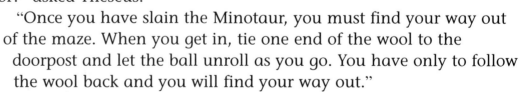

"Then how can you help us?"

"If I can find a way of helping you, you must take me back to Athens with you, for there will be no safety for me in Crete if it is found out that I have helped you."

"Very well. You shall come with us. But how are we going to bring this about?"

Cautiously Ariadne drew a sword from under her cloak and gave it to Theseus.

"It is enchanted," she told him. "No creature can withstand this sword." Then she handed him a ball of woollen thread.

"Take this too," she said. "You will need it."

"What for?" asked Theseus.

"Once you have slain the Minotaur, you must find your way out of the maze. When you get in, tie one end of the wool to the doorpost and let the ball unroll as you go. You have only to follow the wool back and you will find your way out."

Theseus listened carefully to these instructions, and early in the morning the young men and maidens were led to the entrance of the maze. Their guards opened the great bronze door and drove them in. As soon as the door was locked behind them, Theseus bade his companions remain hidden close to the beginning of the maze.

from* Giants and Warriors *retold by James Reeves

2 Role play

In pairs, discuss one of these moments from the story:

* the moment after Ariadne has told Theseus how to kill the Minotaur
* the moment after the great bronze door is closed behind Theseus.

Role play the two characters at that moment. Be ready to tell the rest of the class how your character is thinking and feeling.

3 Using connectives

You can use connectives to speed up the pace of your writing, which makes it more exciting. You can:

* add connectives to join sentences together, for example:

    I was terrified when I heard a strange noise.

* start with a connective and rearrange the sentence, for example:

    When I heard a strange noise I was terrified.

Use these connectives to make this passage more exciting.

if   when   then   but

although   next

finally   since

because   while

meanwhile   as

I was terrified. I heard a strange noise. Then I saw two red eyes. I went into the dark. I could smell him. He was stinking.

I suddenly saw him. He had a sword too. He hit me with his sword. I hit him back. He was much bigger than me. I had a good idea. It was a bit risky.

4 Create your own Greek myth!

1 Plan a new Greek myth based on this story idea:

The King of Athens asks Theseus to rescue a group of five children from the monster you created. Artemis, the goddess of the moon, helps Theseus to defeat the monster.

Make sure you give your myth a beginning, middle and end.

Beginning
Show Artemis telling Theseus about what he has to do.

Middle
Describe the battle Theseus has with the monster, and how he rescues the children.

End
Show Theseus returning the children to Artemis.

2 Use your plan to write your myth.

Remember!

* Use connectives to help the story flow and to create suspense, for example: "suddenly", "without warning".

* Mention your hero's actions, thoughts and feelings.

* Your myth must excite the reader – use powerful adjectives and verbs, particularly in battle scenes.

* End the myth in a satisfactory way.

What I have learned

* I can compare different ways of telling the same myth or legend.

* I can plan and write my own Greek myth, creating my own monster.

* I can use connectives to help the story flow and to create suspense.

* I can write about characters' actions, thoughts and feelings.

Daring Adventures

In this unit, you'll read news reports about young adventurers. Then you'll write your own report, including an interview.

Climbing Mount Everest

This article is about an exciting climb made by two teenagers.

ON TOP OF THE WORLD

At just 19 years old, two daring friends became the youngest-ever Britons to climb Mt Everest. Now they're planning their next big adventure – travelling across the globe. Manpowered!

Best friends Rob Gauntlett and James Hooper had been on lots of cycling adventures, but neither of them had ever done any climbing. So when they decided to climb the highest mountain on Earth, it was no surprise that people didn't believe them!

"We were on the train one day, when we saw a story about an expedition to Everest, and we just thought, 'Hey let's do it!'" says Rob. "People laughed at us when we told them, but you can't let that stop you," adds James. "You have to give them a reason to believe in you and prove them wrong!"

The determined pair began their training. They practised at indoor climbing centres, and then moved outdoors. They had just turned 17 when they set out on their first serious climbing expedition, in the Karakoram mountains of North Pakistan. This finally proved to everyone that they were serious – and on their way to the top!

DID YOU KNOW...?
In Nepal Mount Everest is called Sagarmatha, "goddess of the sky", while Tibetans call it Chomolungma, meaning "mother goddess of the universe".

They didn't just dream it – they did it!

from **National Geographic Kids**

1 Responding to the text

Answer the questions from the , or section.

1. What are the names of the *best friends*, and how old were they when they set out on their first climb?

2. What did people think of their idea?

3. What mountain did they want to climb most of all?

4. Where did the boys train?

5. Find the words *Karakoram mountains*. In what country are they?

1. What things had Rob Gauntlett and James Hooper done together when they were younger?

2. Which is the highest mountain on Earth? What other names does it have and what do they mean?

3. Why do you think the boys decided to go on the journey?

4. What training did they do?

5. Why do you think this training was important? Think of two reasons.

1. What factual details can you find about the mountaineers? Make a fact file like this to display them.

Names and ages:	
Achievements:	
Future expeditions:	
Any other details:	

2. What kind of training did the boys do and why was it necessary?

3. What was their first expedition?

4. What qualities would you say the two boys had? Choose three that are the most important for their expedition.

5. What other names are given for Everest? How do the meanings of these names give us clues about the nature of the mountain?

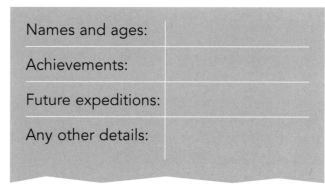

Ocean crossing

Read about the challenge that 14-year-old Michael Perham took up.

HERO OF THE MONTH...

Stories about people setting sail on solo voyages aren't uncommon, but when that person is just 14 years old it's pretty amazing!

Michael Perham set off from Gibraltar on 18th November last year with the hope of becoming the youngest person ever to sail single-handed across the Atlantic Ocean in his yacht, Cheeky Monkey.

On 4th January this year he completed the six-week, 3,500-mile (5,632-km) journey and achieved his dream while also sailing into the record books.

Michael started sailing when he was seven and was trained by his father, an experienced yachtsman, who shadowed him in a second boat through the sometimes difficult journey.

While at sea Michael stayed in touch with his mum by satellite phone and was in radio contact with his dad.

He survived gale-force winds and huge waves but was most challenged by his diet of tinned foods and requested a steak as his first meal back on dry land.

Michael says that while the voyage was a truly great experience the worst bit was being away from family and friends.

Left: Michael Perham
Below: at the helm of Cheeky Monkey

from CY Magazine

2 Responding to the text

Answer the questions from the , or section.

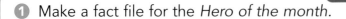

1. Make a fact file for the *Hero of the month*.

2. What was the name of Michael's yacht?

3. What do you think of the hero of the month? Find a word to sum him up.

4. Would you like to do what he did or not? Say why.

1. Make a fact file for the *Hero of the month*.

2. Why do you think Michael Perham was chosen to be hero of the month? Think of the most important reason.

3. Would you call him an experienced sailor? Why or why not?

4. What do you find most surprising about his journey?

1. Make a fact file for the *Hero of the month*.

2. What kind of person do you think the hero of the month is? What do you find most surprising about him?

3. Why is his father important? Think of more than one reason.

4. Sum up what impresses you most about the hero of the month.

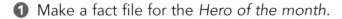

3 Think/pair/share

Look at the picture below, showing a boat in gale-force winds.
Think about what a gale-force wind would be like if you were a sailor.

4 Role play

1. Imagine you're a young sailor sailing in gale-force winds. Your partner asks you two questions about how you feel about the gale. Then swap over.

2. Now imagine you're the sailor's parent. Your partner asks you two questions about how you feel during the gale. Then swap over.

3. Carry out the same two activities with another partner.

5 Write/pair/share

When we say that a piece of writing is funny, sad or exciting, we are describing its mood or tone. Writing can also be formal or informal.

1. Reread *Hero of the month*, then answer the questions from the , or section.

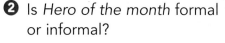

2. Is *Hero of the month* formal or informal?

3. Find four phrases that tell you whether it's formal or informal.

2. Is *Hero of the month* formal or informal?

3. Find two phrases that tell you whether it's formal or informal.

2. Is *Hero of the month* formal or informal?

3. Find four phrases that tell you whether it's formal or informal.

4. Write a list of words to describe the tone of the article.

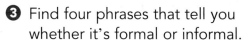

2. Is *Hero of the month* formal or informal?

3. Find four phrases that tell you whether it's formal or informal.

Open and closed questions

When a reporter carries out an interview, they may ask different kinds of questions, depending on what they want to find out.

- A **closed question** will encourage the interviewee to give one answer, for example:

  When is your birthday?

- An **open question** will encourage the interviewee to give a broader answer or more than one answer, for example:

  How did you feel when you made the choice?

6 What kind of question?

Decide whether the questions below are open or closed. Make a note of your answers on a separate sheet of paper or your whiteboard.

1. How old are you?
2. What happens if you change your mind?
3. Why do you think you made the right decision?
4. When did you win your first medal?
5. How might things have turned out differently?
6. How many goals did your team score?
7. Which was your most successful expedition and why?

7 Role play

Work with a partner.

Take it in turns to interview each other.

Ask about which schools each of you have attended and your school experiences.

Remember to use open questions.

8 Preparing an interview

1 With your partner, decide which of these people you want to interview:

- Rob Gauntlett and James Hooper from *On top of the world*
- Michael Perham from *Hero of the month*.

2 Write questions for the interview.

Write six questions. Start your question with one of these words: how, why, what, when, where or which.

Write eight or ten carefully thought-out questions that are a mix of open and closed questions

3 Rejoin your partner. Using your questions, take it in turns to be the interviewer and the interviewee.

Safety and survival tips

Rob and James gave the magazine's readers these tips for staying alive on a climb!

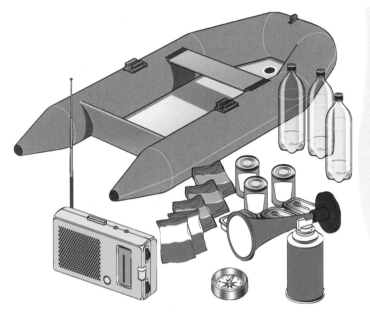

Rob and James' top four survival tips

1. Try curling up into a ball to keep warm.
2. Keep dry. When you're wet, you feel colder.
3. Stay in a group. It's safer than going it alone.
4. Keep calm and stay cool. Panicking won't help!

from National Geographic Kids

9 Writing safety tips

Write your own tips for safety at sea.

Read the list of items below and turn them into tips. Remember, use the imperative!

- life jacket
- radio and spare batteries
- fresh water
- survival rations
- toolbox

- warm, waterproof clothing
- handheld fire extinguishers
- horn with a loud blast
- good ventilation on board

Making longer sentences

Lots of short sentences together can sound boring.

> *Michael set out on his voyage. He knew the sea well. He started sailing when he was seven.*

Make your writing more interesting by using connectives to link sentences together.

> **Before** *Michael set out on his voyage he knew the sea well,* **because** *he started sailing when he was seven.*

10 Joining sentences

Answer the questions from the  or ● ▲ section.

1 Choose from these connectives to put the sentences together.

(because) (and) (so)

a) Rob and James trained hard. They had to be fit.

b) Michael only ate tinned food. His meals were boring.

c) Michael missed his family. He missed home cooking.

1 Make these sentences more interesting by putting them together using connectives.

a) Solo voyages are very hard and long. Michael kept going. He was an experienced sailor.

b) Rob and James climbed Everest. They had been on cycling trips together. They had never done any climbing.

2 Now rearrange the sentences you have made, using the same or different connectives.

11 Planning your report

You're going to write a report that includes an interview. It could be an imaginary interview with a well-known person who has achieved something, or an ordinary person who is in the news for their courage or achievement. It could be a real-life interview with someone in your community.

Remember!

• Include open and closed questions.

1 With your partner, decide whom you'll interview and what you want to find out.

2 Plan and write a series of questions for the interview. Think about:

• why the person is in the news.

• how the person might feel about this.

12 Writing your report

1 Use your questions as a guide to carry out some research. You could:

- interview a real person and take notes.
- make notes for an imaginary interview using the library.

2 Plan your report using your notes.

3 Write a first draft of your report with your partner. Decide:

- what sub-headings to use.
- who'll write each section.
- when you'll share your writing.

13 Editing your report

1 When you have completed your first draft, get together with another pair. Read your reports to each other. Use Checklist 1 on the right to evaluate your reports.

2 In your pairs, redraft the report and proofread it. Use Checklist 2 below to help you.

Checklist 1

✓ Does the report make sense?

✓ Is it generally written in time order? (If not, does it still make sense?)

✓ Does it have paragraphs and sub-headings?

✓ Are connectives used to link ideas?

✓ Is it interesting?

Checklist 2

✓ Spelling – check any words you are uncertain of.

✓ Paragraphs – are they in the right place?

✓ Full stops and capital letters – have all these been included in the right places?

✓ New sentences – do all the sentences stand alone and make sense?

14 Presenting your report

Present your report using a magazine layout and adding pictures and captions. Remember to use some of these design features:

- newspaper columns
- bullet points
- pictures and artwork
- varied fonts.

Remember!

- Write the events of the news story in time order.
- Include time connectives to link paragraphs and sentences.
- Use long and short sentences to give your writing variety.
- Add advice tips or general knowledge information.

What I have learned

- I can identify the features of two news reports.
- I can empathise with the experiences of others through role play.
- I can plan and carry out interviews and research.
- I can write my own chronological reports to a high standard and present my work using magazine design features.

Tales in Verse

In this unit, you'll look at a poem with a story and a poem that has stood the test of time, and write a story poem of your own.

Matilda
Who told Lies, and was Burned to Death

This poem is about Matilda, whose habit of telling lies has dreadful consequences.

Matilda told such dreadful Lies,
It made one gasp and stretch one's eyes;
Her Aunt, who, from her earliest youth,
Had kept a strict regard for truth,
Attempted to believe Matilda:
The effort very nearly killed her,
And would have done so, had not she
Discovered this infirmity.
For once, towards the close of day,
Matilda, growing tired of play,
And finding she was left alone,
Went tiptoe to the telephone
And summoned the immediate aid
Of London's noble fire-brigade.
Within an hour the gallant band
Were pouring in on every hand,
From Putney, Hackney Downs, and Bow.
With courage high and hearts a-glow,
They galloped, roaring through the town,
"Matilda's house is burning down!"
Inspired by British cheers and loud
Proceeding from the frenzied crowd,
They ran their ladders through a score
Of windows on the ballroom floor;
And took peculiar pains to souse
The pictures up and down the house,
Until Matilda's Aunt succeeded
In showing them they were not needed;
And even then she had to pay
To get the men to go away!

It happened that a few weeks later
Her Aunt was off to the theatre
To see that interesting play
The Second Mrs Tanqueray,
She had refused to take her niece
To hear this entertaining piece:
A deprivation just and wise
To punish her for telling lies.
That night a fire *did* break out –
You should have heard Matilda shout!
You should have heard her scream and bawl,
And throw the window up and call
To people passing in the street –
(The rapidly increasing heat
Encouraging her to obtain
Their confidence) – but all in vain!
For every time she shouted "Fire!"
They only answered "Little liar!"
And therefore when her Aunt returned,
Matilda, and the house, were burned.

Hilaire Belloc

1 Responding to the text

Answer the questions from the , or 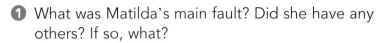 section.

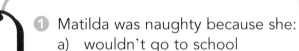

❶ What was Matilda's main fault? Did she have any others? If so, what?

❷ What was the aunt's attitude to Matilda at first? How did it change?

❸ What were the events that lead to Matilda's death?

❹ Why did everybody call Matilda *Little liar*?

❺ Do you think Matilda's aunt was right not to take Matilda to the theatre? Why or why not?

❶ Describe Matilda. Include all her faults.

❷ Describe Matilda's aunt. What were her strengths? Do you think she had any weaknesses? If so, what?

❸ What does the expression "cry wolf" mean? How does it apply to the poem?

❹ What message do you think this story has for the reader?

❺ Do you think Matilda's aunt was right not to take Matilda to the theatre? Why or why not?

❶ Matilda was naughty because she:
   a) wouldn't go to school
   b) told lies
   c) wouldn't get up in the morning.

❷ Matilda phoned:
   a) the fire brigade
   b) the police
   c) the ambulance
   d) all three.

❸ Choose *two* answers that you think are right. Matilda died:
   a) in a fire
   b) because no one heard her screams
   c) because she started a fire
   d) because no one believed her when she told the truth.

❹ Why did Matilda's aunt not take Matilda to the theatre?

❺ Do you think Matilda's aunt was right not to take Matilda to the theatre? Why or why not?

Eldorado

Gaily bedight,
A gallant knight
In sunshine and in shadow,
Had journeyed long,
Singing a song,
In search of Eldorado.

But he grew old –
This knight so bold –
And o'er his heart a shadow
Fell as he found
No spot of ground
That looked like Eldorado.

And, as his strength
Failed him at length,
He met a pilgrim shadow:
"Shadow," said he,
"Where can it be,
This land of Eldorado?"

"Over the Mountains
Of the Moon,
Down the Valley of the Shadow,
Ride, boldly ride,"
The shade replied –
"If you seek for Eldorado."

Edgar Allan Poe

2 Responding to the text

Read *Eldorado*. Answer the questions from the , or section.

●

❶ For about how long has the knight been travelling?

❷ What is he searching for?

❸ Who does he meet? Describe the person.

❹ Do you think he'll find what he is searching for?

■

❶ What is the knight searching for?

❷ About how old do you think the knight was when he started his journey?

❸ How old do you think he is by the end of the poem?

❹ Who does he meet?

▲

❶ For about how long do you think the knight has been travelling?

❷ Who gives the knight advice? Do you think it is good advice? Why or why not?

❸ Why do you think the knight keeps travelling?

❹ What do you think will happen to the knight?

3 It's a mystery!

Answer the questions from the or   section.

■

❶ What kind of place do you think Eldorado could be?

❷ What does the word *shadow* remind you of? Choose from the following:

(sunshine) (a ghost)

(a shady place) (darkness)

❸ Who do you think the *pilgrim shadow* could be? What is he like? Is he good or bad?

● ▲

❶ Where and what do you think Eldorado is? Think of two places and describe them.

❷ Who do you think the *pilgrim shadow* could be? Is he dangerous or helpful to the knight? Describe him.

4 Making notes

You are going to plan your own poem about a mysterious quest in search of something. Think about:

- what you want to write about:
  - Where and why does your journey start?
  - What happens at the end?
  - Do you find what you are looking for or not?

- how you want to write about it:
  - How will you create a mysterious mood?
  - How will you create a strange atmosphere?

- how you will sequence the journey:
  - What places will you visit on the way?

5 Drafting your poem

Use your planning notes to make a first draft of your poem.

You could:

- continue the knight's journey.
- write using "I".
- think about the places visited.
- write using a repeating line.
- use alliteration and metaphors.

Remember!

- Your poem should create a sense of mystery. Choose your words carefully!

6 Think/pair/share

Swap your poems and read them. Discuss each poem, thinking about:

- the journey

- the mood and atmosphere

- pace and volume

- how you will read different parts of the poem, for example the beginning, the end or the repeating lines.

7 Speaking and listening

Practise reading your partner's poem. Perform the poems to each other. How could each performance be improved? Talk about:

- the way you stand

- body language

- changing volume

- changing pace.

When you are ready, present the poems to another pair.

What I have learned

- I understand that writers can tell a story in verse.

- I understand that atmosphere can be created in a poem.

- I recognise the usefulness of drama and role play in understanding a poem.

- I can write a poem and present it.

7

Acting Up

In this unit, you'll learn about how playscripts are written and performed. You'll create a script of your own, using what you have learned, and perform this for the class.

The BFG: In the Queen's Bedroom

This play is adapted from Roald Dahl's The BFG. *The Big Friendly Giant has blown a special dream into the Queen's bedroom window.*

Scene: The Queen's bedroom with a bed and a window. (Curtain up. The Queen is in bed, her crown nearby. It is night-time. After a pause, the Queen's head tosses from side to side as she dreams.)

Queen: (*Talking in her sleep*) Oh no! No! Don't! Someone stop them! Don't let them do it! It's horrible! Please stop them! It's ghastly! No! No! No!

(As she drifts back to peaceful sleep, a tick-tock sound effect suggests the passing of time, and lighting suggests the coming of dawn. There is a sudden knock on the door. Mary, the Queen's maid, enters carrying a tray with breakfast things and a newspaper.)

Mary: Good morning, Your Majesty. Your early-morning tea.

              (*The Queen was up*)

Queen: Oh Mary! I've just had the most frightful dream! It was awful!

Mary: Oh, I *am* sorry ma'am. But don't be distressed. You're awake now.

Queen: I dreamt, Mary, that girls and boys were being snatched out of their beds at boarding-school and were being eaten by the most ghastly giants!

(*Mary pays attention*)

The giants were putting their arms in through the dormitory windows and plucking the children out with their fingers. It was all so...*vivid*, Mary. So *real*.

(*Mary has been staring in amazement. The crockery on the tray rattles.*)

You mustn't take it so hard, Mary, just because I've had an awful dream.

Mary: That...that isn't the reason, ma'am...
(*She reaches for the newspaper*) Look, ma'am! Look at the front page! The headlines!

Queen: (*Unfolding the newspaper*) Great Scott!
(*She reads...*)

"Children vanish mysteriously from boarding-school beds. Bones found underneath dormitory windows!"
(*She gasps as she scans the small print*)
Oh, how ghastly! It's absolutely frightful! Those *poor* children! Mary! What is it?

(*Suddenly Mary drops the tray with a clatter*)

Mary!

Mary: Sorry, Your Majesty...

Queen: I think you'd better sit down at once. You're as white as a sheet.

(*Mary sits on the edge of the bed*)

from Roald Dahl's The BFG – plays for children *adapted by David Wood*

1 Responding to the text

Read this playscript with a partner.

Discuss and then answer the questions from the , or section.

1 Which two words tell you that the play has started?

2 Which words tell the Queen how to move her head?

3 What sound effect is used to tell you that time is passing by?

4 How does Mary know what to do on stage as the Queen is telling her about her dream?

5 Why was Mary directed to *drop the tray with a clatter*?

1 What sound effects are needed in this play? Why will they be used?

2 What props (furniture and objects for use in the play) are required?

3 What has Mary realised that the Queen hasn't?

4 How can we tell this from the stage directions?

5 Do you think Mary and the Queen could have been given more advice on how to speak their lines?

Imagine that you're the director of this play.

Write a list of important points you must remember to tell the actors, props people and lighting crew. The advice you give must be in addition to the stage directions that they already have.

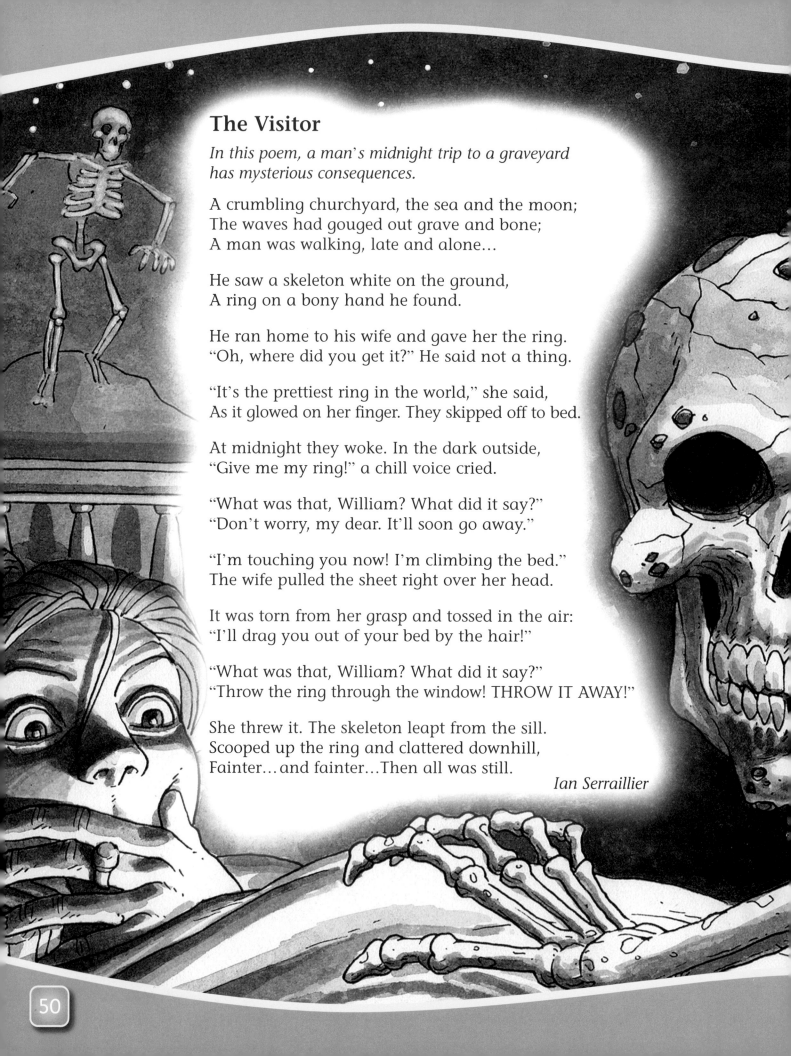

The Visitor

*In this poem, a man's midnight trip to a graveyard
has mysterious consequences.*

A crumbling churchyard, the sea and the moon;
The waves had gouged out grave and bone;
A man was walking, late and alone…

He saw a skeleton white on the ground,
A ring on a bony hand he found.

He ran home to his wife and gave her the ring.
"Oh, where did you get it?" He said not a thing.

"It's the prettiest ring in the world," she said,
As it glowed on her finger. They skipped off to bed.

At midnight they woke. In the dark outside,
"Give me my ring!" a chill voice cried.

"What was that, William? What did it say?"
"Don't worry, my dear. It'll soon go away."

"I'm touching you now! I'm climbing the bed."
The wife pulled the sheet right over her head.

It was torn from her grasp and tossed in the air:
"I'll drag you out of your bed by the hair!"

"What was that, William? What did it say?"
"Throw the ring through the window! THROW IT AWAY!"

She threw it. The skeleton leapt from the sill.
Scooped up the ring and clattered downhill,
Fainter…and fainter…Then all was still.

Ian Serraillier

50

Using storyboards

This storyboard could be used to plan a playscript version for the first part of the poem, *The Visitor*. It shows what happens in a series of pictures and captions, and gives information about sound effects (SFX), props (P) and lighting (L).

Churchyard by the sea

SFX – waves, wind

L – dim, with a spotlight on the grave

P – background scene with grave and skeleton

A man walking through the graveyard.

SFX – crunching gravel

L – dim, with spotlight on man

P – background scene with grave

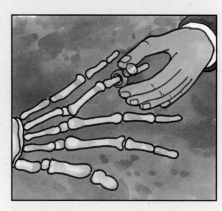

He steals the ring from a skeleton.

SFX – waves and wind

L – dim, spotlight on ring

P – skeleton and ring

2 Planning and writing a playscript

1. Make a storyboard for the rest of the poem, showing what happens when William goes home to his wife. Make notes about the sound effects (SFX), props (P) and lighting (L).

2. Write a playscript based on your storyboard. Include stage directions and put brackets around them. They should show:

   • how characters move, speak and react.

   • lighting and sound effects.

   Start a new line for each speaker.

3 Presenting the play

When you have finished your playscript, get together into groups of four.

- Decide who is going to act in the play, and who is going to direct.

- Decide how you will act out the first part of the play, using the storyboard on page 51.

- Decide whose playscript you want to use for the last part of the play.

- Rehearse the whole play several times, ready for presentation to the class.

Remember!

- Speak your lines clearly so that your audience can understand the words.

- Make your performance interesting for your audience – you could add music and sound effects.

What I have learned

- I can write a playscript based on a poem.

- I can use playscript conventions, including stage directions.

- I can prepare a performance from my own playscript.

The Art of Persuasion

In this unit, you'll look at how language is used to persuade people what to do and how to think. You'll take part in a supermarket campaign, and design brochures advertising a Roman museum.

Don't miss out!

All the advertisements shown here are persuading people to buy something.

50% EXTRA!

Half Price!

Buy One, Get One Free

Mega chips BBQ Flavour

Free DVD with every toy purchased!

1 Think/pair/share

Read the advertisements on page 53. Discuss the following questions with your partner.

- Who is persuading you?

- What do they want you to do?

- How do they try to persuade you?

2 Exploring vocabulary

Use persuasive language to describe a product called "Temptations". The product can be anything you like – but your advertisement must make customers want to buy it.

Remember to add a picture. You can use the words in the clouds to help you.

Descriptive phrases

hot and spicy
sweet and sour
soft and creamy

Nouns

concoction   delicacy
package   wrap   bap
roll   sandwich   dish
panini

Adjectives

appetising   amazing   creamy   crunchy
delicious   irresistible   mouth-watering
savoury   sweet   scrummy   tangy   tasty
unbelievable   yummy   wonderful

Verbs

bite into
experience   flavour
relish   release
savour   sink
taste

Here is an example:

Bite into this delicious wrap and experience the crunchy, creamy filling – avocado, carrot and sour cream with a hint of strawberry. Amazing!

3 Independent writing

Finish this letter of complaint from the giant in *Jack and the Beanstalk* to the police.

Ed-in-the-Clouds
The Castle
High in the Sky

PC Grabbem
Police Station
Little Stalking
Beanshire

10th September

Dear sir,

I am very upset about the disgraceful behaviour of Jack, who visited my castle, without my permission, at least three times last week.

Firstly he...

A persuasive poem

This poem describes the effects of pollution on a puffin colony.

Puffins

The puffins' nests, deep underground,
Are egg-filled, noisy, full of sound.
The sea alive with food they need,
The puffins swim and dive and feed.

The oilslick, like a deadly hand.
The puffins, lying on the sand.
The puffins' nests, deep underground,
Are empty, silent, not a sound.

Ian Larmont

4 Responding to the text

Read this poem with a friend and answer these questions.

- What's the purpose of this poem?

- What pictures does the poet create in your head in each verse?

- Is this a good way to persuade people and children to think about the issue of pollution?

5 Designing an advertisement

Design an advertisement. Add pictures and sound effects if you want to.

You can advertise whatever you want, for example:

(a car)   (a holiday resort)   (a computerised toy)

Don't forget that your advertisement needs to persuade people to buy the product. Think about using:

- powerful adjectives.

- bold font for important words.

- advertising captions – these should be short phrases, using exclamation marks and imperative verbs, saying that if you don't buy, you'll miss a bargain. For example:

  Half price for this week only!

6 Planning a broadcast

Imagine that you have the chance to set up a new club for children. A local radio show has given you three minutes to persuade people that the club is a good idea.

1. Choose from one of the following clubs, or think of your own:
   - free guitar lessons in the village hall for children under 12
   - free art class once a week for children under 12
   - free cookery lessons for children under 12.

2. Plan the content of your broadcast. Make sure you give some good reasons why the club should be set up.

3. Audition each other to see who should read the broadcast. Pick the person with the most persuasive style.

4. Rehearse the broadcast – give your presenter feedback. What are they doing well? What could they improve?

7 Designing a flyer

The supermarket is sending out flyers to advertise the products it'll sell. Complete the following tasks in pairs.

1. Create three new captions for different products to show the wide range of products in store.

2. Create an advertisement for the new coffee shop in the store.

3. Design your flyer, by hand or on screen. Arrange your captions and advertisement, and think of the colours and fonts you want to use.

4. Print off your design or finish it by hand.

Children's clothes

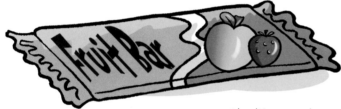

Healthy snacks

8 Writing a protest poem

The supermarket will be built near a wildlife area that has woods, a meadow and a pond.

1. Research which animals, birds and plants might live in the wildlife area. Find out how the supermarket would disturb the wildlife.

2. Write a protest poem, showing what effect the supermarket might have on the wildlife area. You can write out the poem on page 59 and complete the unfinished lines.

Countdown

There are ten butterflies in the air,
There are nine sparrows nesting anywhere.
There are eight rare caterpillars by the wall.
There are seven reeds, waving tall.
There are six…
There are five…
There are four…
There are three…
There are two…
There is one…
Now there is nothing, nothing at all!

modelled on a poem by Jack Prelutsky

9 Presenting your case

There is going to be a meeting in the Town Hall, to decide whether the supermarket should go ahead. Groups for and against the supermarket will be asked to argue their case. A vote will be taken and the chairperson will make the final decision.

In your groups, prepare your presentation for the meeting.

1. Write down a list of reasons why you believe you're right.
2. Decide how to present these in an interesting way.
3. Decide who is going to say what in the presentation.
4. Practise your presentation using the checklist to help.

Checklist for a perfect presentation

- ☑ Keep your hands still.
- ☑ Smile and nod at your audience before you begin.
- ☑ Look around at your audience as you offer your views.
- ☑ Speak clearly and audibly.
- ☑ Speak with conviction, emphasising the important points.
- ☑ End the presentation confidently, with a smile.
- ☑ Thank your audience for listening to you.

The Roman museum

You've received a letter from a new Roman museum inviting you to design two brochures for their opening. Read the letter and the information about the museum. Use them for your brochures.

THE ROMAN MUSEUM

The Roman Museum
Middle Lane
Everytown

Everytown School
Middle Street
Everytown

17th September

Dear children,

We are soon to open our new Roman museum down the road from your school. You probably know very little about this, which is why we are writing to you.

We thought it would be a good idea to ask you to design two brochures – one for children aged between 7 and 11 and one for your parents.

The purpose of the brochures is to persuade your parents, and children of a similar age to you, to visit us when we open.

We have enclosed a fact sheet about the museum with this letter. This is a list of the different things to see at the museum, and the varied activities that children can enjoy. You can use the fact sheet to help you design the brochures.

We would be very pleased if you would take part in this venture. No other schools have been asked.

We very much look forward to receiving your brochures.

Very best wishes,

Helen Wigmore

Helen Wigmore
Museum curator

THE ROMAN MUSEUM

The Roman Museum
Middle Lane
Everytown

Fact sheet

- The museum stands on the site of a Roman villa.

- The museum site includes old walls, the remains of a Roman bath, and a small vineyard for growing grapes to make wine.

- A mosaic workshop has been found in the garden.

- Part of the garden has been restored to the Roman plan, including appropriate plants.

- The underfloor heating system can still be seen.

- A Roman mosaic of a horse has been lifted and placed inside the museum. Another mosaic shows pictures from an ancient myth about Jupiter, the god of rain and lightning.

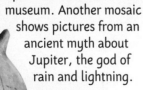

- The museum has a very old Roman statue of a goddess dating from the 1st to 2nd century. It would have been placed in an alcove.

- There is a museum trail.

- There is a Roman word-square scratched onto a piece of wall plaster. No one knows what the words say.

- There is the Roman tombstone of Horatius Optimus, a cavalryman who served in the Roman army for 20 years.

- There are regular storytelling sessions for children.

- A group of actors visits the villa once a month and puts on a show of their riding and fighting skills.

- The museum is open all year round, excluding bank holidays.

- A mosaic workshop happens every week – you can buy some stones and make a picture.

- Every month, a local gardening expert will come to talk about the sorts of plants and herbs that Romans grew.

- There is a quiz for children.

- You can play Roman games.

10 Organising your information

Look at the fact sheet on page 61. The information isn't in any particular order.

Think about how you could order the information under different headings, for example **Outside the museum** and **Inside the museum**.

11 Paired activity

Follow these steps to create each of your brochures.

Step 1: Think about what information to include that will make your reader want to visit the museum.

Step 2: Write six captions about different aspects of the museum. Make them as persuasive as you can – you want the reader to visit the museum!

Step 3: Design your brochure.

You will need:

- an eye-catching front cover.

- a back cover that gives important information about opening times and how to get to the museum.

- well-designed pages – use lots of pictures to match your captions, and lay out your text with your reader in mind.

Remember!

- Write in a style that is appropriate for your reader – the brochure for children will have simpler words and shorter sentences.

- Design the brochure with your reader in mind – the brochure for children will have a larger type size, and more pictures!

What I have learned

- I understand the purpose of persuasive language and recognise it in different forms.

- I can use the features of persuasive writing in interesting ways.

- I can recognise and use both sides of an argument.

- I can produce illustrated brochures aimed at different audiences.

Moving Pictures

In this unit, you'll explore a short film telling the life story of a farmer. Then you'll write your own filmscript, using what you've learned.

The Beauty of Life

The Beauty of Life *is a short, animated film about a farmer called Lars. It follows his life from boyhood through to old age.*

1

2

3

7

8

9

4

5

6

10

11

12

1 Discussing the storyboard

Choose two pictures from the storyboard, one near the beginning and one near the end, and talk about:

- who is in each one.
- what is happening.
- how each picture makes you feel about the characters.

1 Choose three pictures from the storyboard that you think are important. Discuss:

- why you've chosen them.
- where they come in the film.
- the differences between them.

2 Draw up a list of adjectives that you think describe the pictures and the feelings they create. Use a dictionary and a thesaurus to help you.

2 Responding to the text

Answer the questions from the , or  section.

1 Do you think *The Beauty of Life* is about:
a) what it's like to be a farmer?
b) how to draw pictures?
c) someone's life story?
d) a family building their house?

2 Who is the main character in the film?

3 List three things that happen to the main character.

4 What part of the film did you like best? Why?

1 What do you think the film is mainly about?

2 Who is the main character in the film?

3 How does the main character change?

4 Who else changes in the film?

1 Sum up in a sentence what you think the film is about.

2 Name three characters in the film. How do they change?

3 What else changes in the film? List two things.

4 Why do you think the film-makers have chosen the title *The Beauty of Life* for the film?

Bringing the storyboard to life

In *The Beauty of Life*, the story is told in pictures. The pictures have been brought to life by a process called animation. In many animated films, every frame is drawn by hand.

An artist draws the key frames in a sequence.

Other artists draw the frames in between, to complete the sequence.

The camera then shoots the frames in sequence. The film is speeded up and the sequence comes to life. Soundtracks, sound effects and dialogue are added later.

3 Creating a flick book

Bring your own sequence of drawings to life. Create a flick book of the dog with the wagging tail from *The Beauty of Life*. Practise drawing the dog before you start, and remember to keep your drawing simple.

You'll need:

- thin flexible card
- tracing paper
- a strong stapler
- a pencil.

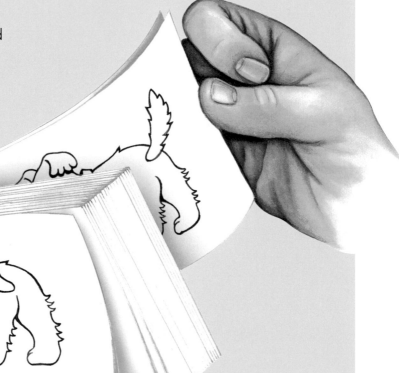

1. Cut at least ten pages out of card to make a small booklet. All pages should be the same size.

2. Staple your book together. The first page is your cover.

3. Draw the dog at the far end of the second page.

4. Draw exactly the same picture at the far end of the third page, but shift the tail a little. (You can use tracing paper for this.)

5. Do the same on the other pages, shifting the tail a little each time.

6. Flick the book with your thumb and watch the tail wag. (Hint: it is easier to flick from back to front.)

7. Design your cover.

8. Now make a flick book using your own idea.

4 Films and stories

1 Think about times when you've read a story and then seen a film of it. Was the film like you imagined?

2 Think about times when you've seen a film and enjoyed it so much that you've read the book. Was the book the same as the film?

3 Discuss the following questions with your partner:

- How is watching a film similar to reading a story?

- How is it different?

5 Meanings of words

1 Write definitions for these key words. They are all important film words.

(producer)　(director)　(scriptwriter)　(soundtrack)　(animation)

2 Think of four more key words to do with film.

6 Think/pair/share

1 Here are some film words. Decide what you think each word means and write it down. Check your ideas in a dictionary.

(best boy)　(gaffer)　(clapperboard)　(swing gang)　(greensman)

2 These words all have two meanings. Write a definition of the everyday meaning for each word. Then write a definition for the film-industry meaning. Use a dictionary to help you.

(grip)　(dolly)　(crew)　(boom)　(cast)　(credits)

Picture metaphors

A metaphor in writing is when a word or phrase stands for something else. For example, "The milky face in the sky" stands for the moon.

A picture metaphor is when a picture stands for something else. For example, during the film, the old man watches geese migrating and the sun setting.

In this picture the old man is sitting on his own. His wife has died. The setting sun and the migrating geese stand for this sad event in the farmer's life.

7 Thinking about metaphors

At the very start of the film, the child draws a picture of himself and his father planting an acorn.

The tree grows and changes as we watch the film.

Look at the pictures with your partner and discuss these questions.

1 What is the link between the acorn and the tree?

2 How does the tree change?

3 What happens to the tree throughout the film?

4 What do you think the tree represents?

8 Role play

Work with your partner. You're going to play the roles of the father and his son from the second still in the storyboard on page 64.

Talk about:

- the setting (for example, are you on the hill or walking up to it?).
- what is happening.
- the kind of things the characters might be saying to each other.
- who will play each part.

Remember!

- The dog is in this scene. Use a prop to represent the dog and talk to him from time to time.

9 Write/pair/share

Write a playscript for your role play. Use the example here to remind you how to set it out.

> opening scene stage directions

Playscript model

A beach with two deckchairs. It is summer, late afternoon. Two children enter. The boy starts searching for something.

> colon after character's name

Luke: I'm sure I left it here – by the deckchair.

Meena: What did you leave?

Luke: *(Worried)* My bag, my towel – and my drink as well. Oh no! My football's gone!

(Meena looks under a deckchair.)

Meena: Well there's nothing. Not a thing.

(Jacob, an older boy, enters carrying a bag.)

> stage direction in brackets in dialogue

10 Creating a storyboard

You're going to plan a storyboard of your own life. It'll show eight scenes.
The first scene will be your birth. The last will be a scene from your recent life.

① Discuss with your partner what scenes you're going to include.

② Make notes about:
- when and where you were born.
- what you can remember from when you were small.
- what you can remember from your life up to the present day.
- a few special moments in your life.

③ Plan your storyboard and make it using art materials. Include eight scenes from your life, with notes underneath each frame.

④ Choose a special moment from your storyboard to create a screenplay. Think about whether it would make a good story, and whether it would work with two characters.

11 Planning a screenplay

Take turns to work through your ideas for your screenplay with a partner. Act out the scenes together, thinking about:
- what happens.
- where it happens (setting).
- who is speaking (characters).
- what they'll say in each frame.

12 Writing a screenplay

① Make a first draft of your dialogue.

② Read it to a friend. How could it be improved?

③ Redraft your dialogue and set it out like a playscript. Think about the directions you would need to add to turn it into a screenplay, for example: lighting, sound effects and camera angles.

Remember!

● Don't choose too many characters.

● Don't give your characters too much to say. A little speech goes a long way.

● Choose one or two settings only.

13 Drama

When you're happy with your screenplays, work with a partner to rehearse and act them out.

What I have learned

● I understand that a story can be told through visual effects.

● I understand that a soundtrack and sound effects can add meaning and atmosphere.

● I recognise that drama and role play are useful to understand and plan a story.

● I can plan a scene and present it as a script.

A Caribbean Tale

In this unit, you'll read a story by James Berry, explore setting, characters and issues, and write your own story about bullying.

Tukku-Tukku and Samson

Tukku-Tukku is the nickname of a boy who lives in the Caribbean. This is his story.

All of the other boys call him "Tukku-Tukku". And this Tukku-Tukku boy doesn't like the name at all.

The name is used slanted, you see. It doesn't only mean he is little and fat; it's used to cut deeper, much deeper. It means he is a "downgrow" boy, a "spoilt-breed" who'll never grow, never be capable, never be anything besides a born spoiler. And in truth, he is dwarfed, smaller than all of us, though the same age.

You can understand why he will die first before he'll have the name "Tukku-Tukku" fastened on him. But, you see, the boy who named him has an endless appetite for mischief. And *he* is tall and sturdy, his arms as good as new steel. He is clean looking like a young prince. He eats good food and sleeps in a clean, springed bed. He wears shoes to school. In class he always has the answers at the tip of his tongue and fingers. He's the best batsman in any cricket side at school. The boys love him. They call him "Samson".

It stands out a mile that Tukku-Tukku is different. He's everything Samson is not.

And Samson thinks he's really peculiar. Tukku-Tukku's face is seldom washed clean. He sleeps on the floor, is half starved, and has no shoes. Granny Tom, his guardian, cuts his hair. And just as she makes his little sister's dresses, the granny makes the clothes that droop and hang about on him. But mostly he is ragged. Most days he's a thickhead at school. No one has ever picked Tukku-Tukku for a cricket side. Yet, don't you ignore him altogether. He is sinewy. He is strong and tough. His pair of little pestle legs and bare feet know every village lane and bush track in the surrounding hills. Fresh air and wild fruit – and a full life of field, domestic and school work – seem to have developed something special in him.

So, man, it is Saturday mid-morning. A brilliant sun is up high. Birds are singing all around. Under the tall trees, only boys are at the spring for water. Everybody knows something is going to happen. Samson is here.

You see, Samson doesn't carry water or wood or tend animals or work in fields or sweep the rooms of his house, like Tukku-Tukku does. His father is the local shopkeeper; also he has big banana and coconut fields and servants and hired hands. And Samson stays late at school studying; he seldom meets Tukku-Tukku on the school road. He goes to school last, swiftly on his bicycle. He often has to put himself out to meet Tukku-Tukku. Sometimes, though, the other boys have it all fixed up smartly, like this morning.

from A Thief in the Village and Other Stories *by James Berry*

1 Responding to the text

Answer the questions from the , or section.

1 If you were Tukku-Tukku, how would you feel?

2 Who gave Tukku-Tukku his name?

3 Which are correct? Samson is:
   a) small for his age
   b) not liked by other children
   c) well-looked after at home
   d) liked by other children.

4 Who does Tukku-Tukku live with?

1 In the text it says that the name Tukku-Tukku *is used slanted*. What do you think this means?

2 What Caribbean words are used to describe the name Tukku-Tukku? Do you know, or can you guess, what they mean?

3 What other words give clues that the setting is not in Britain?

4 Who gave Tukku-Tukku his name? How do you think Tukku-Tukku feels about this?

5 What do you think Samson's personality is like? What clues in the text tell you?

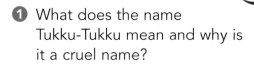

1 What does the name Tukku-Tukku mean and why is it a cruel name?

2 Who has *an endless appetite for mischief*?

3 What are Tukku-Tukku's strengths?

4 Who is Samson? Find two ways in which he is different from Tukku-Tukku.

2 Write/pair/share

Find out about the two main characters in the story by searching in the text.

1. Look at paragraph three. Find words that tell you about Samson. Use a spider diagram to record your words.

2. Find a paragraph that tells you some facts about Tukku-Tukku and record them on a new spider diagram. Remember to add his strengths.

3. Find paragraph seven. What jobs does Tukku-Tukku do? How is this different from Samson's life? Add this information to your spider diagrams.

4. What other paragraph reveals information about the boys? Add these points to your spider diagrams.

3 Exploring vocabulary

Writers often use adjectives to give detail to a noun. They can be used in different ways. For example, you could say:

It's a rich, milky coconut.   or   *The coconut is rich and milky.*

The adjectives *rich* and *milky* give us information about the coconut.

1. Look at this sentence in paragraph three of the story:

And he is tall and sturdy.

2. Find the adjectives in the sentence.

3. Who is the sentence describing?

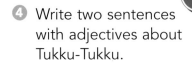

4. Write two sentences with adjectives about Tukku-Tukku.

5. Then do the same to describe Samson.

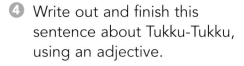

4. Write out and finish this sentence about Tukku-Tukku, using an adjective.

Wild fruit and fresh air meant that…

5. Now write a sentence about Samson, using an adjective.

4 Writing about characters

Write six sentences about Tukku-Tukku to make a character sketch. Begin your paragraph with a topic sentence like this:

Tukku-Tukku lives with Granny Tom. He is a poor boy…

Write a paragraph to make a character sketch about Tukku-Tukku. Begin your paragraph with a topic sentence.

Glossary

character sketch — gives a picture of a character in words

topic sentence — the first sentence in a paragraph; hints at what the paragraph will be about

5 Role play

Work with your partner to play the parts of Tukku-Tukku and Samson. Follow these instructions carefully.

- Decide who'll play each part.

- Decide where the scene takes place (for example, on the road to school or on the beach).

- Role play this sequence:

  Samson jeers at Tukku-Tukku. Tukku-Tukku remains silent. He takes no notice. Samson becomes more annoyed. Tukku-Tukku remains silent throughout. He refuses to get angry.

- Swap roles and work through the scene again.

6 Think/pair/share

When Tukku-Tukku is bullied, he decides to remain strong.
It's good advice, but not always easy to do. It's better if people get along.
How can people do this?

1 Work with a partner. Think of as many positive things as you can that would discourage bullying. Write your ideas down on paper.

For example:

Be a friend to new children in your class.

2 When you have drawn up your list:

- think of a title for it.

- read it to another pair of children, then listen to their list.

7 Talking to Granny Tom

When you want a character to speak in a story, you use speech marks.

For example, imagine this conversation:

"Where have you been, my boy?" said Granny Tom, who was standing at the door.

"Nowhere," muttered Tukku-Tukku.

"You must have been somewhere," said Granny Tom, looking worried.

❶ Read the conversation between Tukku-Tukku and Granny Tom in activity 7. Take a part each. Talk about what Tukku-Tukku's next reply will be.

❷ Write down the reply on your own, using speech marks. Check it with your partner.

Carry on the conversation, writing it down using speech marks. Think of a good reason why Tukku-Tukku is late.

8 Creating your own story

Write your own story about a quarrel or bullying.

Story opening

- Open with a character, and include the character's good and bad points.

- Decide where your story is set and describe the setting.

Problem

- Create a problem for your character, involving another character.

- Think about what your character decides to do.

High point

- Decide how you could make the problem worse.

- Decide what happens next.

Story ending

- Think about how you want the story to end.

- What happens to your characters?

- Is the ending happy or sad?

Remember

- Include some dialogue.

- Include a final paragraph summing up your main character's thoughts.

- Change your plan if you think of new ideas as you write.

What I have learned

- I can read a story that captures the setting of another culture.

- I understand that bullying occurs in all cultures and can be overcome.

- I understand the typical structure of a story: opening, problem, high point, ending.

- I can write an effective story, building on character.

11

Classic Stories

In this unit, you'll read from classic children's books and write an opening chapter to a story.

At the Red-brick-fronted Villa

The three children in this story live a comfortable and carefree life. Then something happens to change their lives dramatically.

They were not railway children to begin with. I don't suppose they had ever thought about the railway except as a means of getting to Maskelyne and Cook's, the Pantomime, Zoological gardens, and Madame Tussaud's. They were just ordinary suburban children, and they lived with their Father and Mother in an ordinary red-brick-fronted villa, with coloured glass in the front door, a tiled passage that was called a hall, a bathroom with hot and cold water, electric bells, French windows, and a good deal of white paint, and "every modern convenience", as the house-agents say.

There were three of them. Roberta was the eldest. Of course, Mothers never have favourites, but if their Mother *had* a favourite, it might have been Roberta. Next came Peter, who wished to become an Engineer when he grew up; and the youngest was Phyllis, who meant extremely well.

Mother did not spend all her time in paying dull calls to dull ladies and sitting dully at home waiting for dull ladies to pay calls to her. She was almost always there, ready to play with the children, and read to them, and help them to do their home-lessons. Besides this she used to write stories for them while they were at school, and read them aloud after tea, and she always made up funny pieces of poetry for their birthdays and for other great occasions, such as the christening of new kittens, or the refurnishing of the doll's house, or the time when they were getting over the mumps.

These three lucky children always had everything they needed: pretty clothes, good fires, a lovely nursery with heaps of toys, and a Mother Goose wall-paper. They had a kind and merry nursemaid, and a dog who was called James, and who was their very own. They also had a father who was just perfect – never cross, never unjust, and always ready for a game – at least, if at any time he was not ready, he always had an excellent reason for it, and explained the reason to the children so interestingly and funnily that they felt sure he couldn't help himself.

from **The Railway Children** *by E. Nesbit*

1 Responding to the text

Answer the questions from the , or section.

① Who are the children in the story?

② Where did they live?

③ What did their mother do with them?

④ What was their father like?

⑤ Would you say the children were happy? If so, why?

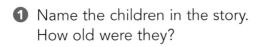

① Name the children in the story. How old were they?

② Where did they live and what sort of home was it?

③ What kind of person was their mother?

④ What was their father like?

⑤ Why would you say the children were lucky?

① Who were the children in the story? Describe them.

② What was the name of the place where they lived? Describe it.

③ Describe the children's parents.

④ Who else was in the family?

⑤ Sum up the children's life in this passage.

Changes Ahead

Here is the next part of The Railway Children.

You will think that they ought to have been very happy. And so they were, but they did not know how happy till the pretty life in Edgecombe Villa was over and done with, and they had to live a very different life indeed.

The dreadful change came quite suddenly.

from The Railway Children *by E. Nesbit*

2 Think/pair/share

Answer the questions from the or section.

1. What word in the last sentence tells you that something is going to happen to the family?

2. What do you think could happen? Think of two things.

1. Discuss what kind of things might happen to the family. Think of three possibilities.

2. Why do you think the writer kept back this important information until later?

3 Drama

Create a scene between the characters Roberta, Peter and Phyllis. It should show how they react when they discover how their lives are to change.

Together, decide:

- what the *dreadful change* will be.
- where the scene will take place.
- who'll play which part and what they'll say and do.
- what props to use.

Remember!

- Although all characters may feel the same, they should react differently!

A Puzzling Picture

In this text from the first chapter of The Little Prince, *the narrator describes a memory from his childhood.*

Once when I was six years old I saw a beautiful picture in a book about the primeval forest called *True Stories*. It showed a boa constrictor swallowing an animal. Here is a copy of the drawing.

The book stated: "Boa constrictors swallow their prey whole without chewing it whereupon they can no longer move and sleep for six months digesting it."

I then reflected deeply upon the adventures in the jungle and in turn succeeded in making my first drawing with a colour pencil. My drawing No. 1 was like this:

I showed my masterpiece to the grown-ups and asked them if my drawing frightened them.

They answered: "Why should anyone be frightened by a hat?" My drawing did not represent a hat. It was supposed to be a boa constrictor digesting an elephant. So I made another drawing of the inside of the boa constrictor to enable the grown-ups to understand. They always need explanations. My drawing No. 2 looked like this:

The grown-ups then advised me to give up my drawings of boa constrictors, whether from the inside or the outside, and to devote myself instead to geography, history, arithmetic and grammar. Thus it was that I gave up a magnificent career as a painter at the age of six. I had been disappointed by the lack of success of my drawing No. 1 and my drawing No. 2. Grown-ups never understand anything by themselves and it is rather tedious for children to have to explain things to them time and again.

So I had to choose another job and I learned to pilot aeroplanes. I flew more or less all over the world. And indeed geography has been extremely useful to me. I am able to distinguish between China and Arizona at a glance. It is extremely helpful if one gets lost in the night.

As a result of which I have been in touch, throughout my life, with all kinds of serious people. I have spent a lot of time with grown-ups. I have seen them at very close quarters which I'm afraid has not greatly enhanced my opinion of them.

Whenever I met one who seemed reasonably clear-sighted to me, I showed them my drawing No. 1, which I had kept, as an experiment. I wanted to find out if he or she was truly understanding. But the answer was always: "It is a hat." So I gave up mentioning boa constrictors or primeval forests or stars. I would bring myself down to his or her level and talk about bridge, golf, politics and neckties. And the grown-up would be very pleased to have met such a sensible person.

from **The Little Prince** *by Antoine de Saint-Exupéry*

4 Responding to the text

Answer the questions from the , or section.

1 What do you think drawing No. 1 looks like? Think of four things.

2 What did the narrator do instead of painting? At what age would he have done this?

3 Why do you think the narrator has *spent a lot of time with grown-ups*?

1 Why do you think the narrator made a drawing of a snake?

2 What did the grown-ups think of his drawing?

3 Why did he make another drawing for the grown-ups?

4 Why do you think he gave up painting?

1 Why do you think the narrator wanted to draw the snake?

2 Apart from a hat and a boa constrictor swallowing an elephant, what else could drawing No. 1 look like?

3 Why did the narrator give up painting? What did he do instead?

The Plane Crash

In the second chapter, the narrator finds himself alone in the middle of a desert.

Thus I lived alone with no one I could really talk to, until I had an accident in the Sahara Desert six years ago. Something broke down in my engine. And since there was neither a mechanic nor a passenger with me, I prepared myself for a difficult but what I hoped would be a successful repair. It was a matter of life and death for me. I had scarcely enough drinking water for a week.

from The Little Prince *by Antoine de Saint-Exupéry*

5 Think/pair/share

Talk about the questions in the or section.

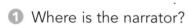

1. Where is the narrator?
2. What must he do?
3. Do you think he'll succeed? Will he need help?
4. Decide what might happen next. Write down the best idea.

1. What do you think could happen next?
2. Think of three things and discuss them.
3. Note down your best idea.

6 Role play

In your pairs, develop your idea and introduce a new character to help the narrator.

Think about:

- where the character has come from (remember the setting is a desert).
- whether the character is a friend or foe.

Role play the scene when the new character arrives, and show what might happen next.

Spoken words

Read this sentence from *The Little Prince*. It shows **direct speech**. Direct speech is placed in speech marks.

They answered, "Why should anyone be frightened of a hat?"

You can write this sentence using **reported speech**. This means the spoken words are reported, so they are not placed in speech marks:

They answered by asking why anyone should be frightened of a hat.

7 Writing what people say

① Here is an example of direct speech.

The boy said, "I have finished my drawing."

Change it into reported speech.

The boy said that...

② Change this example of reported speech into direct speech. Write out the sentence.

The grown-ups then advised me to give up my drawings of boa constrictors.

Using apostrophes

Can you find the apostrophe in this sentence?

The train leaves in 20 minutes so we'll have to hurry.

The apostrophe is used to show a missing letter or letters, like this:

we will → we ~~will~~ → we'll

Its without an apostrophe shows that something belongs to *it*, for example:

That house is damaged – its roof has blown off.

8 Write/pair/share

1. Choose which words need an apostrophe. Write them out with the apostrophe in the correct place. If you're not sure, think about where the letters are missing.

   wouldve   hadnt   Im

   ones   shoes   shes

2. Read the sentences below. Which word should have an apostrophe and which should not? Give a reason for your answer.

   Its not easy to draw well. A good painting will often stand out and its shape and colour will attract the eye.

9 Create your own chapter

You're going to write a chapter for a story using ideas from *The Railway Children*. You'll create your own child characters and describe the new home they go to.

1 Before you start writing, think about the setting. Include words that you think will suit a poor cottage from the past.

2 Think about what characters you want to include. How will they respond to their new home?

3 Write the opening of your story chapter, including some dialogue.

4 Then think about the problem for your characters. This could be something to do with their new home.

- How might the problem get worse?

- How might your characters react?

- How will you end the chapter?

5 Write the rest of your story chapter.

6 End your chapter on a note of tension, so the reader will want to read on. You could end with a cliffhanger – an ending that leaves the reader in suspense because no one knows what will happen next.

Remember!

- Include details about the setting.

- Create an atmosphere using carefully chosen words.

- Describe the characters' reactions to their new home.

- Try to include some dialogue.

10 Read/pair/share

In groups, read each other's chapters. Do the chapters:

- capture the atmosphere of the cottage?
- include dialogue?
- bring the characters to life?
- end on a note of tension?
- use accurate spelling and grammar?

11 Storytelling

Redraft your chapter. Read it to yourself. Then tell it to a partner from memory.

Remember!

- Bring your story to life when you tell it, by using expression and changing your volume and pace.

- You can change your plan. You may think of new ideas as you write.

What I have learned

- I can read from classic stories.

- I recognise that classic stories are set in the past.

- I can write a chapter for a story with an effective setting, using a classic story as a model.

Speaking Aloud

12

In this unit, you're going to read and perform poems, compare two poems with a similar theme, and then write and perform your own poem.

This poem describes a journey on an old-fashioned steam train.

From a Railway Carriage

Faster than fairies, faster than witches,
Bridges and houses, hedges and ditches;
And charging along like troops in a battle,
All through the meadows the horses and cattle:
All of the sights of the hill and the plain
Fly as thick as driving rain;
And ever again, in the wink of an eye,
Painted stations whistle by.

Here is a child who clambers and scrambles,
All by himself and gathering brambles;
Here is a tramp who stands and gazes;
And here is the green for stringing the daisies!
Here is a cart run away in the road
Lumping along with man and load;
And here is a mill, and there is a river:
Each a glimpse and gone forever!

Robert Louis Stevenson

1 Responding to the text

Answer the questions from the , or section.

1. What seems to be *charging along* in lines 3 and 4? Why?

2. Why is the rhythm important in this poem?

3. How is the tramp's mood different from the mood of the poem?

4. What do you think the writer imagines happens on *the green*? What time of year would this happen?

5. What line tells you that the poem was written a long time ago?

1. Does the poem make you feel sleepy or lively? Why?

2. Find a word in the first line that tells you that the train is speeding along.

3. What does the train pass in the second line?

4. Which of these people are in the poem?

    a) a child   b) a tiger   c) a tramp   d) a postman

1. What can the narrator see from the window?

    a) fairies   c) hedges   e) cattle
    b) witches   d) troops

2. What else can the narrator see?

3. What does *painted stations* refer to? Why do they *whistle by*?

4. What are *brambles*? Why do you think the child is gathering them?

5. What does the rhythm of the poem remind you of?

2 Drama

Work in groups to rehearse *The Pow-wow Drum*.

- Read the verses together. Work out what part each of you'll perform.

- Decide how to present the chorus. Will one of you read it, or all of you?

- Think about how you'll present the poem. Will you have actions?

- Will you use percussion instruments to tap out the beat?

- Practise the poem together. Focus on the beat and try to learn your parts by heart. Try to bring the poem to life in your performance.

This poem is about a Native American tribal gathering.

The Pow-wow Drum

Long black braids and silken shawls
Moving side by side where the eagle calls,
Answering the beat of a pow-wow drum
we come again
to dance again

Hey-a, Hey-a, Hey-a, Hey-a, Hey!
Hey-a, Hey-a, Hey-a, Hey-a, Hey!

Leave the dusty cities far behind,
Meet our brothers of the country with one mind,
Travelling from the east, north, south and west
we come again
to dance again

Chorus

Watching close the feet of lightning fly
Fancy dancers free underneath the sky,
Joining in the circle moving round and round
we come again
to dance again

Chorus

Women shining like the morning sun,
Children making rainbows as they laugh and run,
The old and young meeting like they did long ago
we come again
to dance again

Chorus

David Campbell

3 Read/pair/share

Rhyme is not the same as rhythm, but rhyme can help the rhythm move along.

Look at lines 1 and 2 in *From a Railway Carriage*. The words *witches* and *ditches* rhyme because they end in the same sound.

Find eight pairs of rhyming words at the end of lines.

Look at the rhyme pattern for lines 1 and 2 in *From a Railway Carriage*. They rhyme with each other. This rhyme pattern can be written as:

line 1   A

line 2   A

The third line has a different rhyme. It can be written as:

line 3   B

What do you think line 4 is?

Now work out the rhyme scheme for the whole poem.

4 Writing a performance poem

Plan and write your own performance poem about a railway journey.

What I have learned

- I understand how writers use devices such as rhythm, rhyme and simile to create dramatic effects.

- I recognise the usefulness of dramatic effects in performance.

- I can write a performance poem and present it.

Remember!

- Think of interesting things you would *see* from the window.

- Try to make the rhythm *sound* like a train.

- Include rhymes if you can.

- Include similes if you can.

- Your poem should slow down at the end of the journey.